2 MINUTES'
Peace

The late Valerie Gremont. My dear, special fellow
seeker of peace.

First published in Great Britain in 2020 by
Greenfinch
An Imprint of
Quercus Editions Ltd
Carmelite House
50 Victoria Embankment
London EC4Y 0DZ

An Hachette UK company

A CIP catalogue record for this book is available from the British Library

HB ISBN 978-1-52940-941-3

Ebook ISBN 978-1-52940-942-0

10 9 8 7 6 5 4 3 2 1

Designed by Ginny Zeal
Cover design by Andrew Smith
Cover illustration by Lylean Lee
Interior illustration by Andrew Pinder

Printed and bound in Slovakia by TBB

2 MINUTES'
Peace

Everyday Self-Care for Busy Lives

Corinne Sweet

greenfinch

Corinne Sweet is an author, psychotherapist, psychologist and broadcaster. She is the author of several popular psychology bestsellers, such as *Change Your Life with CBT* (Pearson), *The Anxiety Journal* and *The Mindfulness Journal* (Pan MacMillan), *How to Say No, Overcoming Addiction* and *Stop Fighting About Money* (Acorn). Corinne trained on BBC Radio 4's *Woman's Hour*, was a magazine and newspaper agony aunt and a *Big Brother* psychologist. She appears regularly on TV and Radio, collaborating frequently with BBC Breakfast and BBC Radio Scotland. Corinne blogs regularly at www. corinnesweet.com.

Corinne is a psychotherapist at www.citytherapyrooms.co.uk and www.barnsburytherapyrooms.com and is a Registered BACP member. She is a working single mum and has been a meditator and mindfulness user for over 25 years. She is also co-chair of the Books Committee of the Writer's Guild of Great Britain.

Contents

CHAPTER ONE

An Introduction to Peace

What does a moment of peace mean to you?

A quiet moment on the sofa?
Relaxing in a hot bath?
A stroll in the park?
A cup of tea or coffee in a nice café?
Snuggling under the duvet?
Sitting in the garden?
Stroking the cat or dog?
Reading a good book?
Playing an instrument?

Finding Two Minutes' Peace

Peace means different things to different people. Sometimes it's the absence of noise, to others it's the absence of clutter. For many of us, it involves getting out of the house or office and into the fresh air. It often means living harmoniously with a partner, spouse or friends, or simply an absence of conflict at home, on the street and at work.

For most of us finding a moment of peace means having some time to ourselves — to be without ourselves and our thoughts — away from the pressures of life. And, increasingly, it means being able to break free from what goes on in our heads, in terms of repetitive or intrusive thoughts or anxieties.

Of course, modern life is noisy: traffic passing, gadgets beeping, planes overhead, machinery whirring, people talking, TV and radios blaring. We often feel that we can't find a find a couple of minutes' peace anywhere. Yet, it's not only the external interferences we have to deal with. From my experience as a psychotherapist, we have internal 'noise' that we need to conquer, too.

Finding Inner Peace
More and more of us are suffering from anxiety, stress-related issues, depression and addiction as modern life speeds-up. We feel overloaded and overwhelmed, and there has been an exponential demand to learn the techniques needed to find inner calm. A lot of inner noise, which disrupts our attempts to find peace, can come from us holding negative thoughts and beliefs about ourselves. When your mind is whirring with fear, grief, anger and repetitive negative thoughts, sometimes tipping into obsessions, it is difficult to be calm. Yet, there are things we can do for ourselves to help quell the negative thought process and reduce anxiety. This book will explain more about how we can use the techniques of mindfulness to create more peace in our lives and minds.

Living a Peaceful Life

In order to live more peacefully we need to become more aware of our actions, thoughts and reactions, so that we can start to change and break free of old habits. We often put ourselves under pressure to be perfect and hard-working, and that creates a great deal of stress and turmoil. Deciding and noticing that peace is important to your wellbeing will be the first step to putting into practice some new ways of living your life. This book will help you form a more peaceful attitude towards yourself and your life.

Can Two Minutes Really Work?

Taking two minutes to be calm can create a 'valve' in your body and mind. It can help you find peace when you feel overwhelmed, confused or stressed. Just taking a couple of minutes to turn off your phone, put in ear plugs, lie on the floor, or simply stop, can interrupt the constant flow of demands and noise. If you develop the habit of doing this regularly throughout the day, it can help bring down your blood pressure, reduce anxiety, lower your heart rate and, of course, focus your mind.

TAKE A MOMENT

Stop for a moment, close your eyes and listen. What is going on outside, in the room, the building, the street? What is going on in your head? Where is your attention? Notice how your body feels as you become aware of what you are experiencing. Are you tense? Relaxed? Comfortable? Alert? Take in a deep breath through your nose, and exhale. Repeat twice more then open your eyes. How do you feel? More peaceful? Calmer?

Calming exercise

RISING AND FALLING

This can be done sitting or lying down. Get yourself comfortable and turn off your phone. Close your eyes and bring your focus to the middle of your forehead. As you breathe in, think 'rising' and as you breathe out, think 'falling'. Keep your focus behind your forehead as you breathe in and out. Let go of any sounds you hear and allow your jaw to loosen as you breathe. Drop your shoulders and feel your feet on the floor. Keep breathing, deepening the breath as you go. Take a few moments before you open your eyes and set off again.

Breathing exercise

DOODLE-DO

Take a sheet of scrap paper and some coloured pens, pencils
or crayons. Sit comfortably and allow yourself two minutes of
doodling. Start in the middle of the page and just see where
your doodling goes. Enjoy the sensation of the pen travelling
over the paper and let your mind and creativity flow. Take a
second or two to admire your work. Smile. Keep it or screw it up
and throw it in the bin — whatever takes your fancy.

Calming
exercise

Self-care for Peace

Self-care is really about attending to yourself. It's about not waiting to be rescued, being a martyr, or running yourself into the ground. It's about getting to know yourself, working out what you need and giving it to yourself when you need it. It is essential self-nurture and can be achieved by becoming more self-aware. Think what we are told to do on a plane in an emergency — put the oxygen mask on ourselves before helping others with theirs. The same principle applies in daily life: we have to attend to ourselves *before* (or as well as) attending to others.

Productivity Versus Peace

Many of us have been programmed to achieve, produce, work hard, overwork and juggle work and home life on a daily basis. Our constant focus on competing and being productive, being the best, getting on and pushing our limits, often leaves our wellbeing largely out of the picture. Of course, we want to earn, succeed, achieve, but we often do this in a self-punitive way. We almost revel in being martyrs to the cause, showing how driven and important we are. We skip meals, we rush non-stop and we are slaves to the machine and the screen. So it's all too easy to neglect ourselves in our quest for success and reward and to put ourselves last when demand and pressure is building 24/7.

Integrating Self-Care

So, how can you be productive while looking after yourself? Does it mean quitting your job, retreating to the country, doing yoga and dropping out? Well, for most of us that is neither possible nor practical. Yet many of us take out gym membership and never go. Or take up hobbies and drift off after a month. And those new year resolutions are often forgotten by February.

How can we make the changes we need to make to our lives to keep ourselves fit, healthy and mentally stable to deal with the challenges of the modern world? And how can we find peace in the middle of chaos and mayhem, uncertainty and meltdown? We all tell ourselves we are simply too busy, too rushed, too overwhelmed to stop, even for a moment. Yet, if you can stop – even just for two minutes – it can make all the difference, not only to your day, but to your mental state, your wellbeing and your hectic life. You just have to give yourself permission to do it. It's not a waste of time; it's essential.

Peace on the Go

The beauty of a two-minute break is that it can be done anywhere and anytime. You don't have to be sitting in the lotus position in a spa. You can be sitting, lying down, walking, waiting in a queue, in the back of a car, in a taxi, on a plane or train. You might be waiting for an interview, or on a sofa, on a beach, on a bench, even on the toilet – in fact, anywhere (except when driving or using machinery, of course).

We all need to take mental breaks throughout the day. When we feel we've had enough, or are reaching 'full' on the dial, consciously stop and do something else for a couple of minutes. With a little practice this will form part of your self-care regime and will actually help you to get things done. Ironically, stopping and taking a break helps us achieve your ends far more effectively than doggedly pushing on through exhaustion or fatigue.

CALM YOUR 'JUMPING BEAN' THOUGHTS

Visualization

Set a timer for two minutes. Sit comfortably
in a high-backed chair and close your eyes. Visualize your racing
thoughts like jumping beans bouncing around. Focus on your
breathing and let your thoughts bounce in and around your mind,
and then bounce away. Keep focusing on your breathing and let
the jumping bean thoughts cartwheel away.

BUBBLE WRAP POP

Cut off a small square of bubble wrap. When you feel frustrated,
pop the bubbles between your thumb and forefinger. Really press
down, and squeeze. Pop away your frustrations and irritations. You
can even put some in your pocket or bag and pop discretely when
you feel annoyed. You can keep some in the car glove
compartment, and pop when you stop the car. Popping
can be very satisfying and stress relieving.

Energizing
exercise

CHAPTER TWO

Finding Peace in a Challenging World

Today's world is extremely challenging. We are bombarded with news and events 24/7 and it is easy to feel overwhelmed and overloaded. Life can be noisy, scary, unrelenting, screen-centred and buzzing. Everything is moving fast and becoming ever faster, and we are rushing to keep up while staying sane in the face of political turmoil, climate change and social inequality.

We are bombarded by adverts telling us that we need to buy lots of things to make us feel better. This can add to the perception that we need to 'keep up' or strive to be perfect by spending money. We are literally loaded up with life. This chapter will help you to find a balance and achieve moments of peace even when the world around you seems frenzied and chaotic.

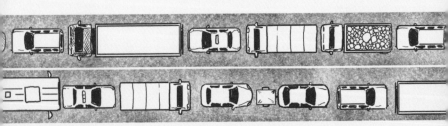

The Good News
The good news is that in the middle of frenzy, frustration
and delay, people are becoming increasingly aware of their human
need for peace and calm. We all need to find a way to connect with
ourselves first and foremost, before we go out into the world. Many
of us bring plants inside our houses, for that necessary 'green'
effect. They're not just pretty, but research shows they absorb
carbon dioxide and exude oxygen, which is good for detoxifying
our home atmospheres. We also know that going outside into the
sunlight, even for just 15 minutes a day, will help us get vitamin D.
This, in turn, increases the release of the 'feel-good' chemicals in
our brains: serotonin and melatonin.

LONG, LOW BREATH

Take a moment to put your hands on either side of
your rib cage. Breathe in deeply, then let out a long,
low blow. Purse your lips, so the air goes out slowly
and deliberately, hissing like you are a balloon letting
out air. Take another deep breath, feeling your ribs
opening as you do. Then let out the breath long and low, like a
deflating tyre. Repeat for a third breath, slowly letting the air out in
a long, slow, hissing, stream — see how long you can make it last.
Sit still for a few seconds, noticing how you feel, before getting on
with the day.

MINDFUL BATHING

When we shower or bathe in the mornings, it is easy for our minds
to be busy making 'to do' lists or going over events of the previous
day. To calm your mind, try to focus on the sensation of washing
your body, stroking your arms, legs, chest and solar plexus with
your hands. Rest your hands on your belly and say to yourself,
soothingly, '*This is me*'. Repeat two or three times. You
might feel a bit self-conscious at first, but this is a
great exercise for connecting with yourself before
you go out into the day. You can repeat '*This is me*'
whenever you wash your hands or bathe.

Breakfast and Beyond

You might be someone who gets up late, rushes to get ready and runs for the bus. Or perhaps you hop on your bike and just make it to work on time. Many of us arrive at work seething after dealing with mind-numbing traffic and/or transport delays. Whatever your commute is like, many of us will forego breakfast in favour of a few more minutes in bed. Yet, having some nourishment before we set off in the morning is pretty crucial to our wellbeing. At the same time, it's common for us to watch TV, listen to the news or check our phones while we eat.

SILENT BREAK-THE-FAST

Turn off all devices, screens, radios and the TV. Sit comfortably and eat your breakfast in silence for two minutes. If you have children try and encourage them to enjoy a few moments of quite time, or calmly explain that you need a couple of minutes' peace and sit separately. Just be with you — taste the food, enjoying the textures and flavours. Savour the moment and enjoy the sensation.

Calming exercise

Setting the Tone

Travelling to and from work can feel stressful. People can push and shove to get onto transport, shout and be rude on the street, and 'road rage' is on the up. We tend to put on headphones to block out sounds or spend time with our heads down staring at our phones, shutting ourselves away in our own worlds. Then, when we look up, we're bombarded by adverts on billboards and public transport. No wonder it's hard to feel serene. However, it's important to feel safe on the street and while travelling, so preparing yourself to travel well is a good place to start.

SMILE TO YOURSELF

Before you set off, take a moment to smile. Research shows that smiling affects your brain in positive ways by releasing neuropeptides, the tiny molecules that allow neurons to communicate. They facilitate the feel-good neurotransmitters: dopamine, serotonin and endorphins. These chemicals are released when we smile and help lower heart rate and blood pressure, as well as lift our moods.

When brushing your teeth in the morning, smile as you finish. If you style your hair or apply make-up, smile in the mirror. As you leave the house, smile to yourself rather than scowl. Not only is this good for your own mood, but it also communicates to others that you are a positive person. By smiling at someone and receiving a smile back, you both release the neuro-transmitting chemicals, so a good feeling is created between you both. A minute or two of smiling to yourself will lift your mood and help you set off on the right emotional track.

Throughout the day try to smile as you meet someone, or before you go into an interview or a difficult meeting. You can smile on the phone (this does transmit as it lifts the tone of your voice to a warm, friendly level), or before you enter a room or meet a group of people. If you have to talk to people, smile as you meet them and it will make a great difference to how you feel, and to how they receive you.

Visualization

Handling Difficult People

We all meet them every day. Those people who
push in front to get on the bus or train, or those who don't
queue at the coffee counter or bar. The drivers who drive their
vehicles right at us and shout obscenities if we don't get
out of their way. Or the people who look a bit grim and
hostile on the street or in a shop or a public place.

How Do You React?

Should you square up and get ready for a riposte, or even a fight?
Do you need a speech prepared, to whip out on all occasions?
Is there a better way to deal with the situation?

If you want a peaceful life, it is best to find a way to respond that does not escalate the situation. And yet, you don't want to be left feeling either abused or that you are a doormat.

Prepare Yourself

The best way is to prepare yourself before you open your front door and go out, get in your car and hit the street. You need to walk tall and be more aware of how you handle yourself in your environment. If you are always using headphones or looking down at your phone, you are blocking out the world and are likely to be less aware of the signals around you and are making yourself more vulnerable. It is important to stay attuned to people and their facial and bodily expressions, as well as your own.

Creative Visualizations

Creative visualizations are pictures we can paint in our minds to help us manage our mental state. Creative visualizations have proved to be extremely effective in lowering blood pressure and improving moods. You simply use your imagination to 'see' yourself as a certain thing or in a certain way. This can be a very effective tool for empowering yourself.

CREATE A PSYCHIC SHIELD

Creating a 'psychic shield' is a great way to prepare for the day ahead and can also be useful during the day when things get tough. Try this two-minute exercise in bed, in the shower, during breakfast, while travelling to work or even in the toilet at work. If the going gets tough during the day, take yourself to a quiet corner for a couple of minutes, close your eyes and take charge.

With your eyes shut imagine an invisible, sparkly cloak in your favourite colour, like one from a fairy tale or the one your favourite superhero wears. Imagine it draped over your head, flowing over your shoulders, down your body, over your knees to the floor. You can see through it, but no one can see you inside it. You are protected.

Visualization

Spend two minutes savouring the colourful sparkles of your psychic shield and feel safe, protected and impenetrable. When you go out, imagine this sheer shield is covering you, fending off any hostile forces or thoughts. Re-imagine it during breaks in the day – you can evoke your psychic shield wherever you are, especially when dealing with difficult people, or when under too much stress from outside demands. This is especially useful if you are challenged on the street, during work meetings or while travelling.

Lunchtime Lifesaver

The days of the long, languid or even liquid lunches
are over for most of us. Lunch is often something in a tub or
paper bag grabbed from a local stall or café, eaten in front of
a screen or skipped altogether. Many of us work through lunch
to meet deadlines or to ensure we can leave on time to collect
children, getting more frazzled as the day goes on.

For our mental health and wellbeing, it is vital to take
a lunchtime break – even for a few minutes. Even walking up
and down the stairs when snatching a snack is good exercise.
Getting some light outside is also important to help us through
the day as it will our help our bodies to boost our immune
systems by producing vitamin D and serotonin. However,
if you have to miss lunch or gobble it down at your
desk, try to get some time away from the office
for a mental break at some point in your day.

STAIR STRETCH

If possible avoid the lift at work and instead take the stairs. This helps to oxygenate the blood, stretch muscles and boost alertness. On escalators, walk up or down instead of staying static. If you can take the stairs over lifts when out and about in shops or wherever, you can gain the energizing benefits.

If you can't get outside the building at work, try to at least find somewhere quiet to get a few minutes' peace. You might look out of a window at the view or pick off dead leaves from an office plant. Even standing in a broom cupboard can give you a break to grab two minutes' peace. This might seem a bit undignified but the mental break will enable you to refresh before getting on with the day.

Energizing exercise

DECLUTTERING

Decluttering is a great way to grab a two-minute mental break during the day. Try decluttering your bag – take everything out and throw wrappings, old tickets and any rubbish into the recycling bin. The act of tidying can provide a nice pause in a day full of demand. You could also declutter your workspace or desk — the act of organizing your papers, pens, jotters and tidying your drawers can help to refresh and organize your mind.

Energizing exercise

LUNCH LIZARD

Lizards are renowned for being able to stop and stay amazingly still, like a stone, for a moment. To help yourself take a break, try finding a quiet corner at work: is there an armchair, a cubby hole, an empty room, even floor space you can use? Put your timer on for two minutes, close your eyes and imagine you are a long, multicoloured lizard, sitting or lying in the sun. Imagine your shiny, iridescent scales, cloaking your body from your snout to your tail. Imagine just being still, on a big hot rock, and soaking up the rays. Keep imagining this until your timer goes off. Take a moment before opening your eyes and coming back to life.

Visualization

Clocking Off and Switching Off

Working hours are becoming longer and longer and some of us will struggle to switch off when we get home. There's a tendency to think that hours hunched over your desk or staring at your screen equals productivity, but most of the current research shows the opposite is true. We actually become less and less productive the longer we spend on our tasks, straining over our desks or workstations, because our brains and bodies get tired and we are no longer effective.

Many people work to very tight time schedules, which don't allow for proper breaks, and this is detrimental to physical and mental wellbeing. Humans are simply not robots, despite the pressure of technology pushing us to act more and more that way.

BACK TO THE WALL

Find a wall space somewhere private and quiet. This might be in the toilets or a kitchen area. You might even have a staff room, corridor or empty meeting room available. Stand with your back against the wall, feet hip-width apart and press your lower back into the wall. As you do, breathe in. Close your eyes and feel the wall at your back. Bend your knees slightly, press your lower back against the wall and breathe. Do this two or three times and then walk back to your desk.

Calming exercise

Coming Home

Arriving home in the evening can be a time of tension
with partners, family and housemates. Couples tend to find
the 're-entry' time when one or both comes home from work
is a tinder-box moment for strife. Homeworkers can't wait to
hand over the children and take a break, while those who have
been out want to rest and chill out, but get handed the kids.
These can be difficult moments to manoeuvre around. Flat- and
housemates may have different habits, and people living alone
may feel lonely, instead of happy once at home after a difficult
day. One person may want to blast out loud music to relax,
while the other wants to sit in the bath, finding some peace
and quiet. These differences need negotiating.

Plan Your De-Stress
We all need to find ways of unloading the day, changing our
mindsets and readjusting for relaxing, family contact, fun or alone
time. Some people set up exercise after work, others go to the
theatre or cinema. Many just head for the pub or bar, or nip into a
supermarket on the way home to get alcohol. Some just need to
'turn off' by watching a series on a screen or listening to a podcast.
It's important for each of us to become aware of what we do to
unwind at the end of a stressful day.

Arguments are common during this time as people are tetchy and
stressed from all the efforts and pressures of the day. Spending two
minutes coming home and chilling out is an excellent idea.

STARFISH STRETCH

When you get home, it's a great idea to take two minutes to lie down on the bed, sofa or floor and stretch out into a starfish shape and simply stop. I call this a 'Starfish Stretch'. You've made it home, and before you start anything else, take a moment to chill. Some people like to change clothes and shower first. But sometimes it's great to lie on the floor, or a yoga mat or even the sofa, floor or bed, and stretch out. You can take a deep breath, and make a guttural noise like 'Ahhhhhhhhhhhhhhh', expressing your relief at being home. Close your eyes and take a few deep breaths, and stay in the moment for two minutes.

Calming exercise

PET SOOTHER

If you have a pet, like a dog or cat, take an animal comb, some kitchen paper and comb through their hair for two minutes. This is a great soother (for you as well as for them, if done with love and care). You can also just stroke them with a sense of awareness, feeling the texture of their fur and enjoying the sensation. Stroking a pet can lower blood pressure and increase your immunity.

Calming exercise

BEACH WALK

This is a great visualization to do to at bedtime. Imagine you are walking along a sandy beach, your feet following the water's edge. You can see the sky, rocks, sand dunes, birds and pine trees along the back of the beach. Focus on the feeling of your toes sliding along the sand, the water on your toes and the sun on your back. Hear the sea coming in and out in soothing susurrations. Keep focusing on your feet walking along the sea edge, one foot in front of the other, with the waves lapping gently. Feel the water, notice the sand between your toes, hear the sea....until you gently fall asleep.

Visualization

CHAPTER THREE

Peaceful Relationships

No man or woman is an island, and we are all dependent on others in one way or another. We experience a wide range of interactions and relationships every day, which can be a huge source of support, care and love, whether romantic, parental, collegiate or friendship. We are all interdependent on a wide range of people – at home, at work, in our neighbourhoods and/or socially – and these relationships form the intricate fabric of our emotional lives. They are essential to our functioning and wellbeing, whether we realize it or not.

We are experiencing more complexity in our relationships than ever before. We live longer, but are more likely to divorce (one in two marriages will break down). Instead of marrying for life, we form, break, reform and create new relationships, so there may be step-families and birth families to 'blend' at different times of our lives. People may change their sexual identities as life continues, which can lead to changes in the way others think about and relate to us. This can all lead to difficulties in maintaining peace in our wider relationships.

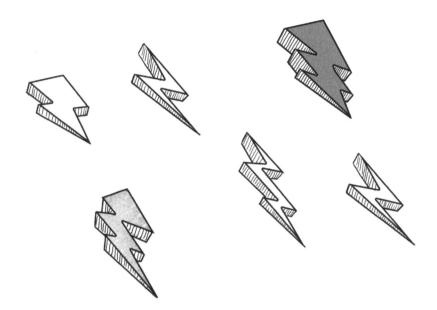

Managing Conflict

There are, of course, times when our relationships
can be taxing rather than helpful, toxic rather than nourishing.
Our relationships can become a source of stress, not least if we
get into a cycle of arguments and conflict. Sometimes our
relationships can become difficult because we are, as
individuals, under stress or undergoing a period of change.
Sometimes the relationships we are in no longer 'fit', satisfy or
suit us. We can literally grow past them as we develop, or we
might feel that we want or need something else and decide
to invite new people into our lives. So how can we make
our relationships more peaceful, while staying
authentic and true to ourselves?

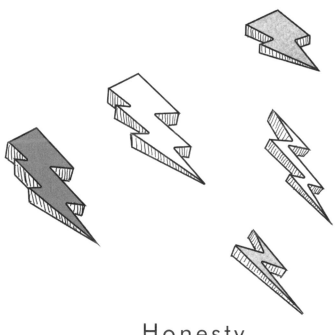

Honesty

To have good relationships we need to be open and honest with ourselves. We need to know what we like and don't like and what upsets us and why, so that we are able to communicate well with others. The more direct and transparent we are, the better our relationships will be. Playing games, or hoping the other person will read our minds, or trying to be what we think others want us to be, often leads to unhappiness and confusion. So knowing ourselves and telling others who we are and what we need is the best route to peaceful relationships. We need to take care of, and understand ourselves, so we can relate well to others.

Handling Expectations

Many people seeking therapy will want to talk about their relationships: they may be upset or angry about someone's behaviour, feel badly treated, they may be questioning a relationship, or dealing with a misunderstanding, such as:

She's driving me mad…it's like talking to a brick wall…

He never listens when I speak…

My boss is never satisfied, always criticising whatever I do…

My partner just doesn't understand me…

The kids keep asking questions over and over, driving me nuts…

My neighbour is always interfering…

She expects everything her own way – she needs to ask what I want for a change…

I wasn't invited by the group, it's not fair…

Unspoken, implied expectations of the other people or person is one of the biggest areas of upset in relationships. We often hope in silence that someone will behave in a certain way and are disappointed when they don't. This can be a huge source of strife. Our expectations evolve from our backgrounds, our religious beliefs, our life experiences, and even our genders.

HOW ARE YOU FEELING?

Mental
break

Take a moment to stop and feel what kind of mood
you are in. Sometimes we disregard our true feelings
and let our heads rule our hearts, or we may have
become detached from our emotions. Ask yourself how you
are really feeling: irritational, bored, annoyed, concerned, lonely?
Try to stop for a couple of minutes to check-in with your mood
several times a day.

Expressing Needs

One of our biggest areas of personal growth is learning
to express to another person exactly what we need from them,
or what we want them to do, without waiting for them to
'double guess' our thoughts or desires and/or read our minds.
This is important for any relationship, be it personal or work
based. The other person doesn't have to agree or comply,
but it is nonetheless important to be able to express
our needs and wants.

PLANT POWER

Set aside a couple of minutes to plant something. Select a cutting or plant that appeals to you and fill a suitably sized pot or trough three-quarters full with potting soil. Make a hole in the soil and pop in the plant, then pat the surface of the earth to level it. Enjoy the feeling of the earth on your fingertips and take a moment to study the cutting or plant. Water the soil and place it somewhere warm and light — a window ledge or greenhouse is ideal. You could also do this with seeds or simply the trimmed leaves from a house plant. The sensation of touching the leaves, patting the soil, watering the plant and tidying afterwards can create a calming break.

Calming exercise

Learning to Level

The art of peaceful relationships is learning how to explain
to other people, calmly, who we are, what we want and
what we need or expect. They may not agree, but we will
probably feel less frustrated and/or misunderstood if we do
some clarifying. This is called learning to level: to express
our thoughts or needs without being manipulative or
getting angry, or going quiet while withdrawing
because we are resentful.

It is important to be appropriate and 'level' with
people in all areas of our lives. We play different roles
with different people, and some relationships work better
than others. We need to think about how we feel about the
significant people in our lives, and then work out –
as coolly and levelly as possible – how to improve
the way we relate to them.

EMOTIONAL BAROMETER TEST

Close your eyes and think about someone with whom you have a relationship — a friend, partner, colleague, boss, neighbour. Now imagine a lift travelling up and down in your solar plexus area, like a bubble in a barometer. Do you get an 'up', airy, joyful, lifting feeling when thinking about this person? Or do you get a 'down', heavy, droopy feeling? This gives an indication for how the other person really makes you feel. It bypasses the conscious, thinking mind and helps us tune in directly to our feelings. The 'up' people are likely to bring positive, mutual, encouraging, heart-warming contact and are definitely worth pursuing. The 'down' people may well need limiting or even eradicating from your life.

Visualization

47

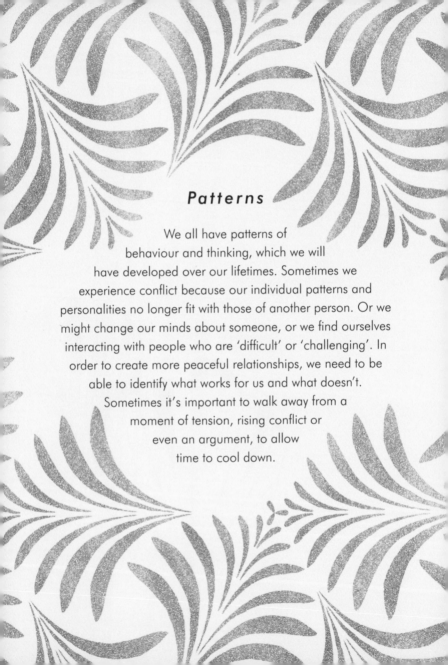

Patterns

We all have patterns of
behaviour and thinking, which we will
have developed over our lifetimes. Sometimes we
experience conflict because our individual patterns and
personalities no longer fit with those of another person. Or we
might change our minds about someone, or we find ourselves
interacting with people who are 'difficult' or 'challenging'. In
order to create more peaceful relationships, we need to be
able to identify what works for us and what doesn't.
Sometimes it's important to walk away from a
moment of tension, rising conflict or
even an argument, to allow
time to cool down.

DEFUSE YOUR ANGER

If you are feeling irritated or wound-up by someone, find a quiet place such as your bedroom, an unused meeting room or even the bathroom. Get a clean tea towel, a small towel, a cushion or roll up your jumper, bury your face into it and roar. Growl into the material and release your frustration for a couple of minutes, before going back to face the person who is annoying you.

Energizing exercise

Boundaries

Boundaries – the place where you end, and the other
person begins – can be a source of tension in relationships.
A lot of unhappiness stems from people invading other peoples'
boundaries by being over-familiar, intrusive or demanding. They
might be too physically close or might even touch you without
consent. It might also be that the boundary is crossed by
too many unwarranted expectations or rules, or by
being too emotionally needy.

SQUEEZE YOUR FRUSTRATION OUT

Energizing exercise

If you are finding it hard to communicate with someone, find a small cushion and go somewhere private or out of earshot. Put your hands on either side of the cushion and squeeze HARD. As you squeeze, say out loud all of the things that are pent-up inside of you. Try this a few times for a couple of minutes. You can also put a big cushion down on a sofa or bed, form a fist and punch it hard, letting out a growl, roar or wail to let your feelings out. Make sure you don't hurt yourself and stay balanced on your feet.

Finding Your Voice

Learning to find your voice, and finding the right physical and emotional distance, is all important for our relationships to be healthy. People feel happier with each other once they know where the relationship boundaries are drawn. However, we can all feel a bit shy or embarrassed about saying what we want or don't want in relationships as few of us are really taught how to relate with confidence. In the bad old days, being polite was seen as all-important. While it is necessary to learn to be appropriate in certain situations, such as at work, it is also important to express our views and feelings in such a way as they can be heard. People often feel unheard, so practising saying your truth is very important.

WRITE IT OUT

If someone is annoying you, try writing a no-holds-barred email or letter, where you say absolutely everything you need to. Swear, blame, attack at will. Describe all of your upsets, grievances, regrets and anger. Rant on the page in pen or type, and really get your anger out. BUT DON'T SEND IT. Instead screw it up and throw it away, delete it, or even set fire to it (safely in the open). You will feel more calm and peaceful having vented on paper or on your screen in private.

Practical exercise

Know Yourself

One of the best tools in building peaceful relationships is knowing yourself well. It may seem obvious, but you need to teach your partner who you are and to do that you need to know who you are. Ask yourself:

What are your likes and dislikes?
What are your wildest dreams?
How do you wish to be treated?
What makes you sad or angry?
Which boundaries do you hold dear?
How do you like to be held or hugged?
Do you want children?
What makes you laugh?
What do you see your purpose in life to be?

ENVELOPE OF POWER

Practical exercise

Write down a list of your ten favourite qualities about yourself. Don't be shy. Put them on a note on your fridge, or in your phone or by your bed. Remind yourself of them whenever you feel a bit down about your relationships. Choose your top three best qualities, write them on a piece of paper and pop them into an envelope. Pull them out whenever you feel discouraged about your popularity or lovableness. Take a moment to connect with these qualities and get to know yourself better, adding to the list every so often.

MUTUAL LISTENING

Practical exercise

One of the biggest areas of conflict in relationships occurs when people simply don't feel listened to by the other person. Ask a person you know well to sit opposite you. You can sit on two chairs or alongside each other on a sofa or bed. First, ask them to speak about something (uncontentious) for a minute. Your job is just to listen. No comment. No jokes. No interruptions. No dialogue. See if you can pay attention to what they are saying. When they are finished, repeat back to them what they just said to you. This is not a memory test, and it doesn't have to be verbatim. However, see if you 'heard' the essence of what they said.

Next, take your turn to talk for one minute and ask the other person to listen without interruption. When you are finished, ask the other person to repeat back to you what you have just said to them. This is a great way of finding out how well you actually listen to each other. Talk briefly with each other about what this task felt like, and what it revealed about your own listening style.

TAKING YOUR MOMENT

If you are finding that relating to other people, handling conflict or even just being in proximity with others is making you more stressed, then 'take your moment' away from them. Go outside and look at the sky — notice the shape of the clouds, the colour of the sky and any trees or birds. If it is night, look for stars or the different colour of streetlights. Enjoy the moment away from others then take a breath before rejoining them. Learn to be comfortable in your own company.

Mental break

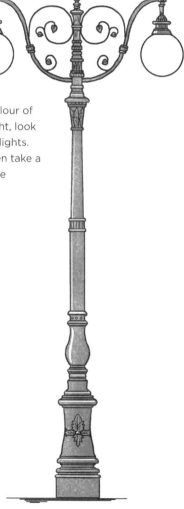

Gratitude and Appreciations

One of the biggest killers of relationships is one or
both people being critical, negative or picky. We tend to
respond best to others who are positive, upbeat and level.
If you find yourself wanting to be critical or negative with
people, it will often push them away or make them wary
of you. Many relationships flounder because one
partner is often negative and seldom says a
good word about the other.

MINDFUL MOISTURIZING

Mental break

After washing your hands, take a dab of moisturizer or hand cream (you can often find it in office toilets and public places, like restaurants, if you don't carry a tube). Put a dollop in your palm and rub your hands and fingers together, slowly and soothingly, feeling the cream smoothing onto your fingers and in between in the cracks and hollows around the nails. Feel the skin soften and smell the perfume. Notice the texture of your hands, the length and shape of your fingers, and enjoy the sensation of moisturizing your skin.

Positive Self-Talk

Negative self-talk can lead to an attitude of self-loathing,
self-neglect and self-hatred. If we get stuck in this kind of cycle,
it makes it very hard to be kind or positive about another
person. After all, if you are negative about yourself (*'I'm stupid'*,
'Nobody could love me' or *'My body is awful'*), then it makes
it hard for you to truly care about another person, in real
terms. You may be equally critical and/or you may idealize
them: both extremes. Neither can lead to healthy,
loving, equal relationships.

Every time you have a nasty thought about yourself
it is important to catch it, wrap it up, and put it in the bin
where it belongs. Holding on to negative self-talk makes it
harder for others to get near to you or love you, as it creates a
shield of venomous veneer around you. Compliments, affection,
kindness and love can veer off the veneer, leaving you feeling
lonely, unloved and discouraged. So learning to love
yourself makes it more possible to be loved by others
(and vice versa).

POSITIVE APPRECIATIONS

Sit for two minutes and make a list of five positive appreciations of a loved one, friend, child, colleague or neighbour. You don't have to share them, but it is important to remind yourself of things that you actually appreciate. If the situation arises, and it seems appropriate, let them know. It will definitely improve things between you if it is heartfelt.

Practical exercise

GIVING AND GETTING CARE

Practical exercise

With your partner or a good friend, agree to spend a few minutes giving some care to each other. You can ask for something you would like: a neck rub, a hand massage, a back rub, a foot massage, to have a story or poem read to you or for them simply to listen while you talk about something important to you. Ask for what you want, enjoy receiving and then swop. This can be a great relationship strengthener.

FINGER STROKE

Take the thumb and forefinger of your right hand and get hold of the base of your left thumb. Pull your fingers towards the end of your thumb in a massaging movement – you can be quite firm to really feel the benefit. Do the same action with the index finger, middle, ring and little finger. Swap hands and do the same with your right hand. Enjoy the sensation of massaging your own fingers.

Practical exercise

CHAPTER FOUR

Peace at Work

Work is a four-letter word that dominates most of our lives. It can seem difficult and challenging to look after ourselves at work, as we seem constrained by external demands and rules. Many of us try to please our employers and feel indispensable, and we often work long hours and overtime. It can be hard, but not impossible, to find two minutes' peace in the whole work arena. It takes effort, but that effort will repay itself a hundredfold.

We spend most of our waking hours at work, and many of us do more than one job or work shifts. Most parents are in work, and women are more likely to work part-time than men. Many parents can end up doing two shifts: the money-earning one, plus the parenting one. Because of daily pressures, it may well be difficult for the main care-giver to find time to rest and relax in either sphere. It can be especially tough to find valuable de-stressing time when you are working and running a family. Finding two minutes' peace will be a real challenge for any working parent.

Being the Breadwinner

It can be hard for the main wage earner in a family
to find time to look after themselves, as they are so often
defined mainly by their work and feel driven to succeed at all
costs. They may have fewer social networks than their partner
who spends more time out of the workplace, and less balance
in life. The pressure to achieve, to compete, to be strong and to
win can override time spent on rest and recovery. Yet many of
us know that our health is impaired by long hours spent
commuting and then sitting at desks without respite.

WALK FAST

Movement is a great way to burn out anger or frustration. If you can go outside and walk fast to the shop or down the road, then walk back as fast as you can. If you can't get outside walk around the room or an office for a couple of minutes. When heading for the station or bus stop later in the day, try to walk a bit faster than usual to help oxygenate your blood and deal with some residual feelings from the day.

Practical exercise

TAKE A MOMENT TO SELF-SOOTHE

Mental break

Find a moment when the children are asleep or during a break at work. Take both of your hands and hold them, palm up, facing your face. Move them over your face so that your fingertips are resting on your eyebrows, and the heel of your hands are cupped under your chin. Close your eyes. Rest your face on your hands this way, eyes closed, for a minute or two. Notice the comforting feeling of your hands, the sensation of darkness, the feeling of resting.

Working for Yourself

Even if you work at home and/or are self-employed —
which is an increasing trend — there will be stresses and
strains to contend with. You will need to set aside time to do
admin, such as invoicing, book-keeping, ordering supplies and
the maintenance of your work area. Your work area might be in
your home or in a shared workspace, so you will need to be
very organized to manage this as well as the rest of your life.
If your work is manufacturing, selling or providing a service, you
will need to be able to research, create and sell
goods. You might need storage space or to find money
for investing in equipment and staff. Finding space
and time for yourself can turn out to be very
challenging indeed.

STRETCH BREAKS

Energizing exercise

It's easy to spend a lot of time hunched over a desk, staring at a screen, driving, on the phone and generally working hard. Put your timer on so that it pings once an hour. Every time you hear the ping stand up or stop your vehicle safely and get out. Stretch your arms right up to the ceiling, feet hip-width apart, and wave your fingers at the ceiling. Keep your knees soft and your head facing forwards. Stretch one arm up towards the ceiling, then the other. Repeat three times.

Stress at Work

For many people work-related stress is caused by:

Commuting by public transport, car, plane etc.
Long working hours.
Being with other people (handling conflict, managing others, being managed, continuously being assessed).
Recovering from work.
Work injuries, such as RSI (Repetitive Strain Injury) from long hours spent at a computer or accidents in the workplace.

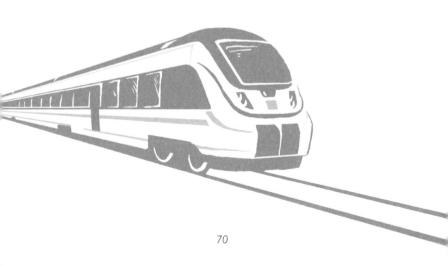

Preparing for Stress

We can prepare ourselves for stress points by anticipating that work will give us satisfaction while also causing us some discomfort. To work out what to do to combat the pressure of commuting, ensure you are allowing yourself enough time for your journey to avoid the stress of being late. Think about how early you need to leave, how to get to your destination and what will face when you arrive. If it's a particularly long journey take snacks and drinks that you will enjoy to keep yourself going – portable cups and snack boxes are great for this.

The more you can prepare the night before – tickets, papers for meetings, agendas, travel arrangements, research about the area, food preparation, appropriate clothing – the more you can help yourself meet the demands of the day without excessive stress.

Screen Age

As we moved from the industrial age to the technological era, the nature and shape of work changed immensely. Many of us are now in the service industries, which means dealing with people, up close and personal, day in day out. There are still many people involved in physical labour, working long hours outdoors, and in the production of goods. However, the majority of us rely on screens in some way or another for our work, be this in offices, call centres, warehouses, on bikes or in vans.

YAWN AWAKE

Turn off your screen and put your phone out of sight. Move away from your desk and find a quiet corner. Open your mouth as wide as you can, as if to yawn, and let the air flow in. You may actually yawn – if you do, let the yawn happen and feel the release. You can make a quiet 'aahhh' sound, like hissing air. Your eyes may water a little but feel how the tension will release from your neck, abdomen and solar plexus. Notice the sensations in your body. Repeat a further six times.

Energizing exercise

NECK STRETCH

Take a moment away from your workstation. Stand up straight, rotate your head to the right and look over your right shoulder. Then slowly rotate your head to the left and look over your left shoulder. You may notice stiffness or clicking in your neck as you do so – be aware of the sensations. Repeat at least four times, stretching carefully all the while.

Practical exercise

Human Pace

Many people now work on zero hours contracts,
which give no job security or time off for sickness, childcare
or even lunch. Working for six or seven days without a break, or
for long hours, means we can be tempted to work for
exceedingly long periods, which is detrimental to
our health (and the welfare of others).

PUTTY SCULPT

Most of us will have a lump of adhesive putty
or similar in our desks or at home. Take a chunk
about the size of a ping-pong ball and soften it
in your hands. Enjoy the sensation of squeezing
and working it into a softer form. You could stretch it, mould it, pull
it, make a shape, then collapse it. Enjoy playing with it for two
minutes and see what you can make. A cat? A banana? A bucket?
Anything you like.

Mental break

HOLD YOUR OWN HAND

If you are feeling worried about the next day, or about the day
ahead or are feeling anxious before a meeting or a presentation,
take a moment to hold your own hand. Clasp one hand in the
other, as if you are shaking hands with yourself, and simply sit, lie
or stand for a minute of two. Close your eyes and feel the
sensation of holding your own hand in a firm clasp. Squeeze
your hands together a little and feel the firmness of your
own grip. Feel the texture of your skin, the strength of
your fingers and enjoy the sensation. You can even
do this under the desk during a difficult meeting, an
appraisal or while giving a presentation.

Calming exercise

Learning To Look After You

The lack of structure in our lives often means that work happens night and day, around the clock and in multifaceted ways. Humans have to adapt to shifts or deliver under tight scrutiny and to strict deadlines. As we prepare for a robotic age, we are being pushed to work in an increasingly robotic way even though we are human, and therefore fallible and in need of flexibility. In order to look after ourselves we need to remember to work at a human pace and take regular short breaks. Our time-poor schedules and lives mean we are rushing, racing and running, often with very little space in between. This can be appallingly disruptive for our diet, sleep, mental health and general wellbeing, so we need to be vigilant against the pressures of our work era and ethos.

CLENCH YOUR FISTS

Energizing exercise

Stretch your arms out in front of you, then bring them in towards you. Face your fingers and thumbs down towards the floor and clench your fist. Squeeze tight, then let go. Squeeze again and let go, then repeat for a few minutes.

FIND A FLOWER

A great way to de-stress is to look at a flower. This maybe in a vase, in a public place, in a garden, or even a picture if you haven't got a real one. Pick a flower you like or a new one you don't know, and really look at the shape and colour of its petals. You could keep a potted plant, such as an orchid, on your desk or workstation so you can look at it from time to time. Notice the colours and shapes of the petals, leaves and stamen. Memorize or draw it, if you like. Enjoy the visual feast and smell it if it's a real flower. Revel in the amazing power of nature to create such a beautiful thing.

Mental break

Social Media

The dominance and pressure of social media as a
main means of communication, along with texting and
messaging, means that for many people relating socially is via
a screen. We are losing our skills of talking on the phone, letter
writing and communicating effectively face-to-face, all of which
were good ways to deal with the issues of the day.

Think Before You Post

We have all become too reactive on social media, and once we have responded it is difficult to undo what we have posted. Take time to deal with your feelings and think of a more measured response. Remember that anything posted on social media or in a chat thread can go viral and will be around for a very long time, if not forever.

If you are feeling upset or angry with someone or something, step away from the screen and take a minute to deal with your feelings. Try not to be instantly reactive. Go away from what you have just seen or read and take some time to process your emotions. Later you might need to go to the gym, go for a run, attack the garden with shears or mow the lawn to work out the anger, but in the short term pummelling a cushion or going for a fast walk around the block can help.

DIGITAL DETOX

Take a couple of minutes away from your screens. Switch everything off and just 'be'. Don't listen, read or watch anything. See how it feels to be quiet and unstimulated while just being with yourself. Breathe.

Calming exercise

Caffeine

Many of us wake ourselves up with caffeine
and use it to keep ourselves pepped-up at work all day.
Workplaces tend to have coffee flowing all the time, and it's
very easy to feel wired, jittery, exhausted or irritable by the end
of the day. This is because caffeine stimulates the adrenal
glands and we end up with insulin pumping away in our bodies.
Try taking some decaffeinated tea or coffee to work, or herbal
teas, so that you have your own alternative drinks. You can
easily take sachets or teabags to meetings and ask for hot
water – this is perfectly acceptable and will help to keep
your stress levels down.

NOTICE A VIEW

Take a moment to stop and look around you — is there a view? If you are at your desk or on a bus or train, look out the window for a few seconds. If you are driving, pull the car in safely and look around you. If you can't get to a window, look at a view on your screen for a minute or two – choose a photograph you took or a picture that appeals to you. Notice the colour of the sky, the trees, the shape of any buildings. Are there any animals? People? Colours? How does the view make you feel? Does it remind you of anything? Is it somewhere that means something to you? Take the view in and enjoy the mental break from your work.

Alcohol

It's tempting to have a swift beer or a glass of
wine at lunch, and some businesses seem to rely on liquid
lunches to build and bond relationships. It's not unusual to be
offered alcohol at meetings, launches and conferences. It is
always thought that alcohol helps events to flow smoothly,
largely because it lowers our inhibitions and makes people feel
more friendly towards each other. However, we all need to be
aware of our alcohol intake during work events, not least to
prevent us from saying or doing something we might later
regret. This becomes even more true in the after-work drinking
culture or the Christmas party that ends all Christmas parties,
where people lose control. You may find yourself wanting
to have drinks after work, but be mindful of how
often you go, or how much you drink.

Alcohol and Work

Although it's great to bond with colleagues, remember that alcohol is a depressant, not a stimulant, and if you get home worse for wear you will spend the evening, night and the next morning recovering. Not to mention the hangover and loss of focus and productivity the next day. You may even lose a whole day of work while you recover.

Drinking is expected in many cultures but drinking too much and too often is not good for the liver, kidneys and brain (remember that the World Health Organization now takes the view that there are no safe alcohol limits). It is easy to slip into drinking too much, especially after work or at events with free booze, so we all need to remain aware.

Drink Aware

If you want to watch your alcohol intake, try non-alcoholic beer, wine or cider, or mocktails. They have the advantage of looking, feeling and even tasting like their alcohol-containing counterparts but without the negative effects. Alternate alcoholic drinks with soft drinks or water and try to keep count of your units. Remember that drinking coffee does not actually sober you up, especially not enough to drive, operate machinery or look after children safely.

Notice if you are using alcohol to deal with stress of work, or if you are drinking to be one of the gang. You can still go to social events and have a good time while staying relatively, if not totally, sober. You may even impress your employer by being first at your desk and the most productive the day after.

Live to Work or Work to Live?

Many of us work to live and can't wait to plan the next
day off or book a holiday. However, an increasing number
of us simply live to work and that means letting work dominate
our waking hours. This can mean not seeing your children grow
up or missing key moments in family and social life. Learning
to look after your physical and mental health needs is crucial
if you are someone who overworks as a norm, as eventually
your health may break down and your personal
relationships will bear the brunt.

SLOW BISCUIT NIBBLE

Mental break

At work there are often biscuits available and it's all too easy to munch on them without thinking. Try using a biscuit break as an opportunity for a mental break. Look at the biscuit and notice its shape and texture, then eat it slowly to allow the flavours to melt on your tongue. Notice the textures, the tastes – are they on the back or front of your tongue? Is there fruit? Chocolate or cream? Is it crunchy or does it melt in the mouth? If you dunk, watch what happens and notice how it now tastes.

Energizing exercise

ROLL UP, ROLL DOWN

If you are feeling a bit stiff or tired, or in need of a stretch, find a quiet corner and stand with your feet hip width apart. Tuck your chin into your neck and roll down towards the ground, vertebra by vertebra, letting your arms hang forwards. Go as far as is comfortable, then come back up, vertebra by vertebra. Pause and note how you feel. Repeat twice more.

Booking Me Time

Look at your calendar. Is it packed with meetings or chores? Or full of things you have to do for others? Is it a constant social whirl? Are there are any times where you are just with yourself? Do you ever block out space just to 'be'? If you find it difficult to find time for yourself you might need to block out time, as you would for a meeting, to allow time to do something you enjoy. It might be physical, or even time to just be quiet and switch off.

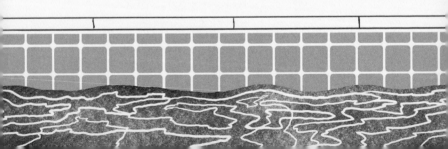

Try putting in at least two hours a week of empty
space just for you – just start with one if that's all you can
manage. You can go for a walk, watch a film, go to the gym,
visit a garden, go swimming or even just sit quietly looking at
the sky. It's essential for your physical and mental wellbeing to
put yourself high on your own agenda, away from the
constant pressures of work.

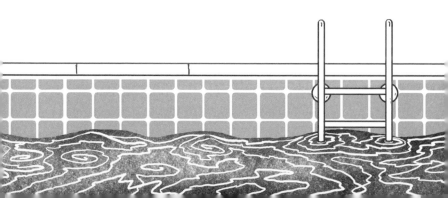

CHAPTER FIVE

Peace in Times of Change

Change is inevitable in life. Many things are constantly changing, and very few things stay the same. While some people feel excited and enlivened by change, others may resist change or even find it threatening. Everything we experience in life changes as we travel forwards: our relationships, our cultures, our own physical features, our growing children, our neighbourhoods, the political system, the world environment and, of course, ourselves.

Fear of Change

It's common for people to want to hold back change at all costs. This is usually caused by fear: fear of the unknown, fear of being caught out and fear of change itself. However, if we accept that everything changes, and that change is natural and inevitable, then it may be easier to survive in times of uncertainty. Change is to be embraced, but it takes time, effort, intention and ultimately determination, to succeed.

Change Paradox

We often say that we want to change x or y, but real change takes effort and may involve changing a pattern of behaviour, breaking a habit or adopting a way of thinking. Change means change, but we often hope (secretly) that we can change without having to change. This is the change paradox: I want to change, but do I really want to change enough to have to change (my diet, habits, way of living, way of thinking, beliefs, etc.)?

Enjoying Change

Once we set a goal and start working towards our
changing habits and patterns, we often feel a surge of
confidence and power – change suddenly seems possible and
desirable and it can be empowering. The fear that surrounded
the idea of change begins to melt away, and we begin to feel
calmer. Hence, it is possible to find some peace in the middle of
transition and change: it's a matter of attitude, effort and
remembering to take frequent mental health breaks.

CUCUMBER COOL

Get two slices of cucumber, or a damp flannel, and lie on a bed, sofa or on the floor. Close your eyes and place the cucumber over your eyes or the flannel over your eyes and forehead. Take a couple of minutes to enjoy the cool, dark sensation as you relax. Notice how it feels.

PAPER PLAY

Take a sheet of scrap paper. Fold the bottom left hand corner up to the top edge to create a triangle leaving a margin of paper on the right side — cut this off or fold it and tear it off. You should now have a folded triangle. Fold the triangle in half again to make a smaller triangle. Cut or tear holes and shapes along the folded side, including the point. Unfold the paper and see what you have made. Colour it in, or stick it to your computer or on the wall as a reminder to take a break.

Significant Life Changes

Significant changes can create the most stress for people. Sometimes we are facing multiple changes at the same time, such as 'coming out' while finding a new job or divorcing and moving house. Obviously, the more changes we are going through at any one time, the more stressed we will probably feel.

The following are changes that are typically stress-inducing:

Moving house

Renovations

Getting engaged

Getting married

Separating

Divorcing

Work deadline

Job interview

Changing jobs

Changing work pattern

Redundancy

Setting up a business

Returning to work

Retirement

Coming out

Gender identity transition

Menopause

Children leaving home

Death of a loved one

Overcoming an addiction

Starting therapy

Relocating

Travelling

Infertility

Miscarriage

New baby

Bankruptcy

Starting university

Chronic medical condition

Disability

Family conflict

Political change

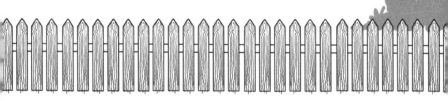

HOW YOU FEEL ABOUT CHANGE?

List five significant life changes you find the most exciting, and five changes which are the most threatening or challenging. Think about changes you have already faced and those that may arise in the future, e.g. under *Exciting* you might include moving house, starting a new job or travelling; *Frightening* changes may be divorce, bankruptcy or relocating. It's important to know what you feel about certain life changes, so that you can feel empowered when or if you are confronted by these changes.

Practical exercise

CAT AND CAMEL STRETCH

Do this at home, in the park or garden, or find a quiet space at work. Go on all fours and arch your back, like a camel's hump. Tuck your head down and your tail under as you do this. Then drop your spine and bring our head and tail up towards the ceiling, like a cat. Alternate between the camel and cat five or six times. Move slowly and consciously and don't stretch too far. Notice how you feel in your body and mind afterwards.

Calming exercise

Finding Peace during Change

Finding peace during change is possible.
Here are some suggestions to help you find calm
among chaos and transition.

Research

Find out all you can about the change that is happening to you, or
that will happen. You can research online, read books and talk to
other people who have been through similar experiences.

Support

Talk to friends and family about what is happening to you. It's often
best to talk to people selectively, and maybe find someone who
can empathise with your experience. Sometimes even talking to a
stranger can help — there may be a specialist organization you can
contact or a support group you can join.

Accept

Many of us resist change as we feel threatened by it, or we want to deny it. If we can adopt an attitude of acceptance, it will help us feel more peaceful, even when we are in the middle of trying to get used to a new way of living, relating or thinking. Accept that there will be an inevitable time of transition, when you might well resist and even fight change.

Adapt

Humans are hugely adaptable and we can usually find a way of familiarizing ourselves with the change or transition we are faced with in ourselves or in another person close to us.

Ask for help

If you are finding that dealing with an imminent or actual change is very hard, there is always help available. You can go to your doctor who may refer you for psychological support, or you can talk to a counsellor or psychotherapist, who can help you over the emotional hump of change. See Resources on pages 158–9.

THREE WISHES

Find a nice wide bowl and fill it with water. Light three floating candles one at a time. As you do so, make a wish for a positive outcome to your change or transition and set the candles, individually, onto the water to float and burn. Take a few moments to reflect on your wish.

Visualization

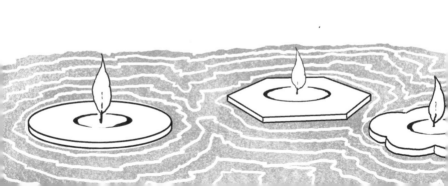

SPOT THE COLOUR

Take a moment away from everything you are thinking about and doing. Notice one colour — say red, purple or yellow — and see how many objects in that colour you can see around you. Try to find ten objects and say them out loud to yourself.

MUSICAL INTERLUDE

Find a portable instrument: recorder, maracas, harmonica, ukulele, guitar, saxophone, whatever you have at your home. Explore it for a minute. Shake it, blow it, make a noise. Have you played it before? Strum or beat a rhythm or hum. If you have no access to an instrument, see if you can whistle. Put your lips together and blow – see what happens. Blow in, blow out and experiment with different sounds.

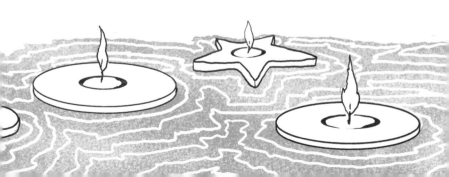

FIND THE POSITIVES

When change is imminent or happening to us unbidden, it is easy to slide into negative thought cycles. We can scare ourselves with the prospect of change, because it is the unknown. Take a moment to think about the change you might be facing or are aware of and make a list of five positive things that are occurring due to your transition or change.

Practical exercise

RUB YOUR FOREHEAD

Calming exercise

Run both of your index fingers along the top of your eyebrows. Start at the temples and work inwards. Work back along the eyebrows to the temples, pressing slightly. Do this three times to release tension and headache.

IMAGINE YOUR CHANGED PATH

Gather together a piece of paper and some coloured pencils and pens. Draw a cave. In the cave, draw three objects that represent the change you are facing or experiencing. Sit back comfortably and visualize the cave and the three objects. Imagine picking up the objects and walking down a path while holding them. See yourself walking quite far down the path, carefully holding the objects in front of you. Notice how you feel as you walk. Notice your surroundings. You come to a rock and put down your objects carefully. You look at them. You have arrived. Open your eyes and take a moment to notice how you feel.

Visualization

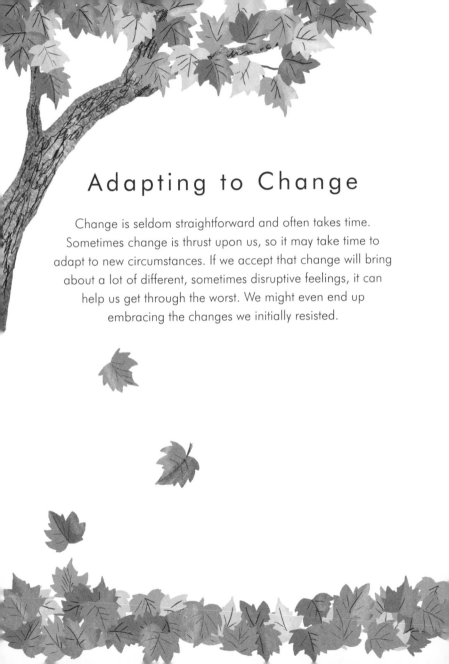

Adapting to Change

Change is seldom straightforward and often takes time. Sometimes change is thrust upon us, so it may take time to adapt to new circumstances. If we accept that change will bring about a lot of different, sometimes disruptive feelings, it can help us get through the worst. We might even end up embracing the changes we initially resisted.

Practical exercise

CLEARING THE LEAVES

If you have a garden or outside area, try clearing dead leaves or pulling up weeds for a couple of minutes. Wear gloves if you need to and keep a trug or bag to hand. The fresh air, exercise and sense of achievement can help to lift your mood. Put the leaves or weeds onto the compost heap (ask a neighbour if you don't have one). Do some clearing whenever you need a break.

CHILD STRETCH

Energizing exercise

Find somewhere you can kneel in private. Sit back on your heels, lean forwards and stretch your arms out in front of you, hands palm-down on the floor. Feel the stretch in your lower back. Come up for a few seconds, then go back and stretch again. Do this three times. Notice the relief in your body afterwards.

Keeping a Journal

Keeping a journal of the changes you are facing, in a book or on screen, can help to chart the emotional journey and also help you to learn from the experience. You can read it back at a later date and wonder how on earth you got through it all. You can also see the self-care exercises you employed to keep yourself going, who you turned to, the things that were useful, and those that were not. This is good information to have to hand for when you meet your next life challenge.

Practical exercise

WRITE IT DOWN

Treat yourself to a beautiful writing book and pen, or set up a screen journal of some kind, and take time to notice how you are approaching your change. Note down your emotions, your thoughts, things that are helping, the people who are supporting you, those who are not and what you have learned. Your journal is a roadmap of how you have dealt with the change and how you have found peace.

ALL IS WELL

Sit or lie comfortably on your bed, sofa or yoga mat. Make sure you are warm and won't be disturbed. Set a timer for two minutes, close your eyes and breathe. As you breathe in deeply say to yourself *'all Is well'*, then breathe out slowly and say *'life is good'*. Continue breathing in and out with *'all Is well'* on the in-breath, and *'life is good'* on the out breath. Continue until the timer goes off. Sit for a moment before continuing your day.

Calming exercise

CHAPTER SIX

Peace in a Crisis

It may seem a contradiction in terms to find any kind
of peace during a crisis – but it is both possible and necessary
for our wellbeing. Of course, crises create the opposite of
peace: they disrupt our day-to-day lives, put us on 'red alert'
and make us feel anxious and afraid. It may be difficult to think
about finding peace in a crisis, but peaceful moments are
possible, even in the middle of difficult experiences.

Occasional crises are part of life and are to be
expected from time to time. The unexpected happens and we
suddenly find ourselves in the middle of mayhem. Without
warning our worlds can be turned upside-down.

Wellbeing in a Crisis

Crises can be extremely traumatic, and because of this, it is important to adopt some kind of self-care strategy to survive and remain calm. We often go headlong into a crisis, only to find later on that we are totally exhausted and spent. It may be difficult, but if you can take a couple of minutes here and there even during a major crisis, it will help you to sustain yourself and recover better afterwards. Mental breaks will allow for a moment of respite, which is essential when the heat is on and you need to find some peace.

Fight, Flight or Freeze

When the unexpected happens and we are caught unawares our bodies start reacting immediately. This is a hard-wired autonomous reaction; in other words, our blood starts pumping faster and our hearts race, to enable our muscles to move faster (so we can run away and escape). We take in oxygen to fuel our potential escape and we start panting or even hyperventilating. Our bloodstreams fill with adrenalin and cortisol, and our brains start working overtime, ensuring our survival. This 'fight, flight or freeze' reaction happens without us having to think about it; it is part of our human life-saving equipment. It enables us to run away when we are being chased, to be alert, to be able to fight back.

Super Strong

People often report suddenly finding huge amounts of strength when under threat, as adrenalin takes over. Some people freeze and can't move, but everything in the moment is recorded in their memory second-by-second. For some, the fear is too great and their memory blacks out or mis-stores information, protecting the mind from emotional and sensory overload. We are all different, and it is important to get to know yourself and how you react in a crisis. The more you understand about yourself, the better you can handle situations when they get out of control. Ask yourself if your most likely reaction is to:

Stay calm

Panic

Shut down

Fight

Take the lead

Run away

Unfortunately, we are living in uncertain times when the news is often grim, and horrific crimes are being committed daily. We are regularly exposed to distressing news reports and images about terrible incidents. This in itself may well keep us in a state of ready awareness when we go out and about. We often have no idea how we would react in a serious situation...until it actually happens.

Handling Anxiety During Crises

We are living in an anxious age and anticipation of what might happen next can fuel anxiety. People are increasingly aware of feeling on edge, jittery and nervous. On the one hand there is a greater openness in talking about how we feel – it is no longer shameful to admit to feeling uncomfortable or even depressed. While on the other hand a crisis is often something we dread happening – and yet if and when it does, it can be possible to find incredible inner strengths.

Some people talk about finding out in a crisis that they have:

Resilience

Determination

Endurance

Bravery

Insight

Ability to connect

While others find crises overwhelming and are left feeling panicked and afraid. It is important to know how you react so that you are well-equipped for meeting the unexpected in life. Even if you are someone who freezes and finds it hard to think in a crisis, it is possible, with time and training, to become more able to react positively and with impact.

NOTE YOUR STRENGTHS

Take a minute or two to jot down ten things that make you strong. Think of adjectives such as 'calm', 'quick-thinking' and 'cool under pressure'. Make a list of your positive qualities that come out to play when you are challenged.

Practical exercise

Endurance

Sometimes crises go on for a long time. At other times
they are intermittent. It is important to get some relief from the
constant stress. We often feel worst once a crisis is over, and
all the adrenalin and cortisol has drained away. When the
pressure is off, we can feel exhausted, depressed and sad.
So it is important to find comfort from taking regular,
peaceful self-care breaks.

Emotional Fallout

It's very normal to feel a wide range of emotions during and after a
crisis, especially if the crisis endures for a long time. There's bound
to be a need to cry, to process what has happened, to withdraw or
to try and blank out feelings. Some people get very irritable or
angry, others may sulk. Try and monitor your feelings and don't
blame others. Notice the emotional fallout and try and use
strategies to alleviate your stress: a massage, a run, more sleep,
less alcohol, good food, etc.

COLOURING IN

Colouring-in geometric or complex patterns has been found to soothe our minds and help us unwind from long periods of endurance and frustration. Buy or download some patterns, get some lovely pens or pencils and enjoy pressing the flow of colour into the defined spaces. Luxuriate in the colours and the feel of the pen on the page.

Calming exercise

Know Yourself

Think of a time when you were under threat, actually
in danger or caught up in an incident – how did you react? Can
you find a positive quality in your reaction? Were you effective?
Are you proud of yourself? Even if you are not a superman or
woman, it is important to give yourself some
credit if you acted decisively and with integrity. If you
have found something hard, can you be
compassionate towards yourself?

Practical exercise

NEEDLEWORK

Needlework is calming, portable and low-tech. You just need a needle, thread, some cloth and your imagination. Try learning some simple embroidery stitches, such as cross stitch or chain stitch, from a book or online tutorial and make patterns on clothing with lovely coloured thread. Or learn to darn a patch on your jeans or a sock. Try a simple flower, or even embroider your name or an affirmation.

LISTEN TO MUSIC

Mental break

When you need a mental break put on your headphones and listen to your favourite track with your eyes closed. If it's a dance track, you could whirl round your bedroom, living room or an outdoor space. Really let go, let rip and enjoy the beats to the full.

Aftermath of Shock

If you have been through a crisis, it will take time
to get over the shock. Sometimes you might experience trauma,
and you might need some specialist help to deal with that (see
Resources on pages 158–9). Make sure you get plenty of rest
and good-quality sleep and try not to self-medicate with alcohol
or drugs. If you begin to have nightmares, night sweats,
flashbacks, panic attacks, shakes, rages or want to drink or take
drugs more frequently, seek help immediately from a medical
professional or call a helpline – there is no
shame in getting help.

WRAP YOURSELF UP IN COLOUR

Lie down on the sofa, floor or bed. Close your eyes and breathe in and out slowly. Imagine you are wearing a thin, shiny suit from top to toe, like a wrapped vegetable. Starting at your toes imagine the colour of the suit in strips:

Toes to ankles: green

Ankles to knees: blue

Knees to hips: orange

Hips to belly button: yellow

Belly button to chest: purple

Chest to neck: white

Neck to the top of your head: silver

Open your eyes and see how you feel.

Visualization

Calming exercise

BATH SOOTHER

If you are feeling jittery or afraid, try a nice hot bubble bath or shower. Sink into the water or appreciate the cascade of water on your skin, and focus on your breathing. Think, 'I am alive' when you breath in, and 'I can relax' when you breathe out. If you have a partner or spouse, or good friend with whom you feel intimate and safe, ask them to soap your back or sit with you while you bathe or shower.

LIE DOWN AND RELAX

Take a moment to lie down and really tune in to your body, starting at your head. Relax your eyes, nose, mouth, ears and neck. Move down the body, relaxing your shoulders, arms, chest, torso, stomach, hips, bottom, thighs, knees, calves, ankles and finally your feet. As you do, think of a colour flowing from the top of your head down to the tip of your toes.

TELL YOUR STORY

An effective way of dealing with shock and trauma is to tell your story. You might want to tell it verbally to a trusted friend or counsellor, you might want to write it down or even attempt to draw it. Do whatever you need to do to spell it out and explain what happened, how you feel and any lasting effects. You may need to do this several times over to clean up the trauma altogether. However, your story will always leave a trace and you should not be worried by that – it's entirely understandable and normal. Notice how you feel after writing things down.

TASTE TEASER

Prepare a favourite snack, such as a piece of fruit, a slice of cheese or a square of chocolate. Suck it slowly. Let it disintegrate on your tongue. Savour it. Take time to enjoy the food teasing your taste buds.

CHAPTER SEVEN

Peaceful Wellbeing

How do you feel?
How healthy are you?
Do you look after your body?
How can you look after yourself better?
Is there a link between your physical wellbeing
and mental state?
Are you at peace with your physical self?
Do you like your body?
Do you take care of your appearance?

How Are You?

Many of us feel permanently 'under the weather'. We may have aches and pains, feel stressed out and constantly have colds. We may also use everyday addictions such as smoking, alcohol, drugs and unhealthy food to mask our emotional problems, which can lead to chronic physical conditions. When we start working emotionally, we peel back patterns of behaviour and thinking, and often discover that we are being hard on ourselves physically as well as emotionally. The result can be poor physical health, which in turn can lead to poor mental health.

Health Anxiety

The other end of the spectrum from self-neglect, health anxiety is a hyper sense of awareness of any physical issues. People experiencing health anxiety may spend a lot of time and money on treatments, and/or worry constantly about being ill or dying, to the point where it has become a huge, debilitating preoccupation. The first step to finding peace in this situation is for people to get a more balanced view of themselves and to take care of themselves in a realistic, unanxious way. If fears or symptoms persist, it's time to consult a medical professional.

SHREDDING HEALTH ANXIETY

Make a list in a thick black pen of all the things you fear is wrong with you physically. Take the list, screw it into ball and throw it in the bin or shred it. See how you feel afterwards.

Practical exercise

MELT PAIN

If you have an ache or pain, sit quietly and focus on it. Breathe and imagine your breath floating into the core of the pain. Imagine the source of the pain as pink, clear, healthy tissue. Keep focused on the pain as you breathe and imagine the area to be relaxed and healthy. Keep focused as you melt away the pain.

Visualization

Self-care

Increasingly, research is showing that there is a huge connection between what we do with our bodies, how we treat ourselves physically and how our psychology operates. We know that a calm mind will help to keep us fit and healthy because we will be free from debilitating levels of anxiety, and the physical issues that are connected with it.

Attend to Yourself

There is a huge amount we can do to promote our wellbeing by becoming more aware of ourselves and our needs and making sure we take time to 'attend to ourselves'. Taking a little time every day to focus on ourselves can have a positive impact on our health, both physical and mental. Ask yourself:

Am I providing my body with adequate nourishment?

Am I getting enough exercise?

Am I happy with how I present to others?

Do I like my style or am I stuck in a rut?

Are there any complementary health treatments I'd like to explore?

SILVER HEALING SHOWER

Visualization

Sit or lie comfortably. Imagine you are standing
under a shower with silvery light coming out of it
instead of water. Imagine the silvery light flowing over
your head, down your body, soothing and cooling as it flows.
Imagine this as healing light, washing away your worries, aches
and woes from top to toe. Check out how you feel afterwards.

Somatic Illness

An anxious, overloaded mind can lead to the physical manifestations of stress and distress – we tend to somatise (or make physical) our emotions and can therefore experience psychosomatic symptoms as a consequence. This largely depends on personality types; some people absolutely thrive on stress while others find it utterly overwhelming.

Type A or B Personality?

Type 'A' personalities love the pressure of a deadline, while Type 'B's like to take things at a much more level pace and hate feeling stressed. It is important to understand your own personality type and how it may affect your body and your mind to give you the knowledge, and therefore the power, to keep yourself healthy and and calm as possible.

Somatic Symptoms

Migraine

Irritable bowel syndrome (IBS)

Back ache

Stiff neck

Flu-like symptoms

Asthma

Immunity issues

Chronic pain conditions

Chronic fatigue syndrome (ME)

Addiction

Insomnia

Sufferers of somatic illness might spend years trying to treat their symptoms with medication or submerge them under habits and patterns of self-neglect or even self-abuse (like addictions). This kind of approach usually backfires long-term as the underlying psychological and emotional issues need to be remedied to help the body heal itself.

Know Yourself

Acknowledging that our physical symptoms can have a psychological component is the first step towards sorting out physical problems that may well be having a detrimental effect on our day to day lives. Many of us take our health for granted unless or until something goes drastically wrong. We often have a sense that we are pushing ourselves to the limit in some way, or ignoring warning signs, but we hope that we can somehow push on regardless.

When we are young it's easy to use and even abuse our bodies, and not really take care of our health. However, by the time we are in our twenties and working, and moving through life (and towards mid- and later-life), we can gradually become aware that we need to treat our bodies like the wonderful sacred vessels that they really are.

MIRROR MIRROR

Find a mirror or imagine one. Look at yourself
(or imagine looking) and say to yourself *'I am
beautiful just the way I am'*. Keep saying this,
quietly and serenely, for a couple of minutes. If you
have negative thoughts or start getting critical, turn those
thoughts into butterflies that flutter away. Return to *'I am beautiful
just the way I am'* as a daily mantra every time you have a negative
thought about yourself, your body or your appearance.

Visualization

ADORN YOURSELF

Making an extra effort with your appearance is a great way to
boost self-esteem. Styling hair, pressing clothes, applying make-up
and wearing fragrance can help us to feel good about ourselves.
This is not an exhortation to go out and spend money on new
clothes and cosmetics – it is about making an effort and
adorning yourself. Sometimes it's great to experiment
with colour, too. If you've worn black for years, try a
splash of red, amber or purple and see how it feels.
Adorning yourself is a way of saying *'I like myself – I
accept you can like me, too'*.

Practical
exercise

Finding Balance

Achieving a healthy work/life balance can be the key to reducing physical symptoms and recurring illnesses. However, this can be difficult to find and sustain, given the pressures of daily life and our lifestyle choices. Many of us are firmly on work and family treadmills and find attending to our physical needs and wellbeing slips right down the list of priorities. It can become unhealthy food eaten on the run, caffeine all day and then alcohol and/or drugs after work and at home. No wonder we can end up feeling exhausted, hungover, sedentary or even toxic.

GOOD HEALTH GRATITUDE DIARY

It's easy to take your health and wellbeing for granted – we may not really notice how fit and healthy we feel until something goes wrong. If you pull a muscle or become debilitated in some way, it's easy then to realize how much you took your regular fitness for granted. So why not keep a good health gratitude diary as a reminder. Each day, jot down three things you are grateful for: a good appetite, legs that allow you to run, no headache, whatever strikes you. Notice how you feel. If it is a positive feeling, be aware of it and grateful for it. If it is negative, think how you can treat yourself to improve your physical wellness (rest, stretch, go for a walk etc.).

Practical exercise

Habits

Breaking bad habits – such as relying on junk food, smoking or drinking too much and getting too little rest – takes effort. It may be difficult, but it is possible. They key to breaking habits is adopting new ways of doing things and a level of awareness that treating our bodies and minds without respect will ultimately lead to physical collapse. As human beings we need fresh air, exercise, screen-free time and space in between our commitments to sleep and refresh mentally. We also need to nourish ourselves with good food and plenty of water – we are what we consume.

QUICK BODY CHECK

Lie down somewhere quiet and close your eyes. What sensations are you aware of in your body? How do your muscles feel in your legs, abdomen, solar plexus, back? How stiff are your shoulders? How do your arms feel? Is your jaw tense? Open your mouth and stretch your jaw. Feel the floor, bed or sofa under your back and buttocks. Is your stomach gurgling? Is your head aching? How do you feel? Contemplate these feelings for a few minutes.

Holistic Therapies

Over the past hundred years or so, the use of
holistic, natural therapies has gradually crept into
western consciousness and practice. A holistic approach
involves treating human beings as whole physical and
emotional entities, instead of concentrating on individual
conditions or ailments. Rather than a substitute for science-
based allopathic medicine – essential for treating life-
threatening and chronic conditions – holistic therapies can often
be used in conjunction with conventional treatments. Indeed, it
is the search for something to compliment conventional
treatments often leads people to follow a holistic approach.

Therapies to Try

Looking at human beings as whole entities, as integrated neurological and physiologically complex structures, means we can begin to effect changes to our physical wellbeing by altering our states of mind. And we can also change our state of mind by paying better caring attention to our physical state. The following therapies follow a holistic approach and can work wonders to improve general wellbeing or in conjunction with conventional medicine (always consult your doctor to check for any contraindications):

Yoga

Massage

Meditation

Traditional Chinese medicine

Acupuncture

Reflexology

Reiki

SAVOUR AN AROMA

Find a lovely perfume, oil or aromatherapy essence, like ylang-
ylang, bergamot, patchouli, sandalwood or lemongrass. Take a sniff
and really let the smell permeate your senses. Allow it to waft, or
put it on your wrist, rub it in and let it warm. Enjoy the changing
perfumes, enjoy the sensation of smelling. Savour it.

Sensory
exercise

TASTE WATER

We are encouraged to drink water, but do you ever taste it? Fill a glass or bottle with water, still or sparkling, and take a sip. Actually taste it. What does it taste of to you? Try a different kind of water, perhaps a mineral water — can you taste a difference? Hold the water in your mouth — what happens? How does it taste? See what happens with different quantities too, try a sip versus a gulp. Enjoy and refresh.

Energizing
exercise

GRASS WALKING

If you get a chance, try walking barefoot on grass for a couple of minutes. Make sure there is no glass, thistles or dog poo around, then let your toes feel the cool grass between them and really feel your feet on the ground. Walk around for a minute or two, enjoying the sensation. See how springy the grass feels under your feet. Enjoy being outside in the air and greenery. Even during colder weather, a few minutes outside can be great for your energy levels. The more you notice how good it is to be alive, the more motivated you will be to look after your physical wellbeing and be at peace with yourself.

BELLY BREATHING

Sit or lie somewhere comfortable, or even park up the car in a layby. Breathe in deeply and breathe out. Close your eyes. The next time you breathe, let your abdomen relax so your breath goes down deep into your belly. Imagine the air is travelling down a dark tunnel. Feel your belly expand, then expel the air slowly. Try this three times, deepening your breath as you go.

Practical exercise

CHAPTER EIGHT

Peace of Mind for Life

Imagine feeling completely calm and happy. Envisage yourself waking up with a feeling that it's great to be alive, and then going through your day being nice to people and untroubled by any difficulties or challenges. Imagine feeling loved and emotionally stable without a worry or anxious thought about anything. Imagine never shouting at the children, feeling irritated with your partner or getting bored at work. And every time you catch sight of yourself in a mirror rather than focussing on the negatives you think *'Ah, I look great, just right!'*

Looking After You

Learning to notice your moods, your feelings and your upsets, and doing something to help yourself to take a break, is incredibly important for peace of mind. Learning to be calmer despite everything, is about treating yourself as if you are a precious object (which of course you are), and a unique human being. Attitudes of self-punishment, martyrdom and masochism will only lead to pain and exhaustion.

Finding peace of mind can be achieved by taking responsibility for your mental health, for your wellbeing and knowing you have the right to stop and rest when you need to. Destructive behaviours – such as hurting yourself with drugs, drink and unhealthy food – are not the route to peace and happiness. You have a choice to take care of you, to help yourself find a peaceful place in a hectic world. It is possible. What's more, it is necessary.

Giving Yourself Stress

Many of us have a deep desire to be calmer and
happier version of ourselves, but in reality our struggles
with self-doubt hold us back. Our lives can often seem to be
a mass of problems that we need to solve, or issues we need to
work out, and we can give ourselves a very hard time: worrying
endlessly about what people think, whether we are alright, how
to fit in, whether we can measure up. We can worry, too, about
things we have done and said, or the things we haven't done
and haven't said. We can be plagued by our thoughts and
driven mad by endless 'to do' lists. To stop giving ourselves
stress we need to halt the critical, judgemental voice,
which tells us we are not good enough.

ASSUME THAT YOU ARE GOOD ENOUGH

Visualization

Rather than criticising yourself, switch this around and assume that you are good enough. Assume that you are okay, that you are lovable and loved, and that you can be at peace with yourself. Repeat, 'I'm good enough' in your mind.

QUIETEN YOUR MIND

Close your eyes and sit or lie comfortably for two minutes. Notice the sounds around you on the street, in the room or the building, without reacting. Notice what happens as you listen. Do you tense up? Are you relaxed? Let the sounds float over and around you and quieten your mind by letting the sounds float away.

Calming exercise

Four Pillars of a Peaceful Mind

Many of us are full of self-doubt, anxiety, fear or self-loathing. We long to be happy but can't accept or forgive ourselves. At root, many of us feel unlovable and imperfect, and simply find ourselves unacceptable. The Four Pillars of a Peaceful Mind can help to combat this and allow us to begin to find ourselves generally more appealing.
The four pillars are:

1. *Accept imperfections*
2. *Believe you are good enough*
3. *Reduce expectations*
4. *Put yourself first*

I LIKE ME

Make a list of ten things you like about yourself. These could be physical attributes, such as 'I like my strong shoulders' or 'I'm lucky to have curly hair', or personality traits: 'I'm a good listener' or 'I can make people laugh'. Put them in your phone, on the fridge or your desk — somewhere they are visible — and refer back to them whenever you feel self-doubt creeping in.

Practical exercise

PEACEFUL ME

Sit or lie comfortably in a private space. Focus on saying to yourself, 'I am happy, I am well, I am at peace and I am loved'. Repeat several times. See how you feel at the end.

Visualization

Accept Imperfections

By our very nature, human beings are imperfect.
And yet we strive constantly for perfection, despite it
being unattainable. We strive to have the body beautiful,
to overachieve and to be perfect. As a consequence we put
ourselves in a mental torture chamber. The first step to personal
peace is accepting that we are human: imperfect, fallible and
prone to making mistakes. We need to reframe our mistakes
as learning experiences – there is no such thing as a mistake,
just as there is no such thing as a perfect human being. Once
we begin to accept our imperfections, we will be on the first
step towards inner peace.

Believe you are Good Enough

Being a 'good enough' person means that you can begin to value the things you can do and stop focusing on the things that you can't. Being a good enough parent is important, and being a good enough employee is desirable. You need to notice what you can do well and learn to respect it. Being good enough removes a great deal of stress from life and allows you to experiment and explore.

Reduce Expectations

High, unspoken expectations of others, and of ourselves, can be very destructive. Expectations can lead to assumptions, which in turn can lead to disappointment if not fulfilled. Often in life, in relationships, in work, in family and love, we have hidden high expectations that we want others to fulfil. We think that somehow this will make us happy, but it often does the opposite, as we are left disappointed and disgruntled, and certainly not at peace. It is VERY important to explain to others what you expect, what you want, what you need, but not to tyrannize others with these demands. Ask yourself why you have these expectations. Where do they come from? What do they do for you?

Put Yourself First

A great deal of anxiety and unhappiness comes because
we fail to look after ourselves. We often secretly hope that
someone else will put us first, and when they don't, we become
disgruntled and angry. A habit of self-care is an important step
on the road to putting ourselves first. We need to notice when
we are tired, hungry, too hot, too cold or unwell and take
responsibility for it. All too often we push aside the reality of our
feelings as we have a job to finish, a house to run, a boss to
impress. In fact, we end up feeling worse as we have not paid
attention to ourselves and our wellbeing. The result is
unhappiness, unfulfillment, stress and lack of peace.

Creating a Peace-of-Mind Habit

Peace of mind is a habit we can develop, like any other.
Peace of mind means accepting ourselves, being good enough
and perfectly imperfect. It also means taking full responsibility
for our own wellbeing and health – when we begin to do this,
we experience less anxiety. If we can manage our feelings,
fears, moods and outbursts, we feel more in control
in our lives. This means we ultimately feel powerful,
calm and in charge.

Peace of mind means not sweating the small stuff, not
regretting, not giving ourselves a hard time, not becoming
obsessed with things, not ruining a day because of a missed
train or not getting a job. It's about picking ourselves up and
knowing we can move on, calmly, to the next things despite
feelings of emotional upset. It's about giving ourselves time to
recover when we feel bad, resting when we feel tired, eating
when we are hungry, sleeping when we are tired.

It's about being kind to ourselves as we would
be towards someone else. It's about giving the good
things to us – because we deserve it.

NOSE AND MOUTH BREATHING

Sit or lie comfortably and close your eyes. Breathe in through your nose, and out through your mouth, saying 'haaaaa' as you do. Repeat, slowly, three times. Then reverse; breathe in through your mouth, and out of your nose. Which worked best for you? You can experiment with putting a thumb against one nostril and breathing in and out of the mouth. Open your eyes and see how you feel.

Breathing exercise

SWEEP THE PATH

Take a broom and/or a dustpan and brush and sweep your front path, or garden path or your kitchen floor, getting the dirt out of those nooks and crannies. Sweep it up, then stand back and look at your handiwork. Notice how you feel after a short burst of exercise to clear an untidy area.

Energizing exercise

FIVE SENSES EXERCISE

Calming exercise

You can do this alone or with a friend or partner.

Notice five things you can see. Pick something you don't usually notice, or haven't noticed before, like the wallpaper or the sofa colour.

Notice four things you can feel, like the wind on your skin, or the feel of the seat under you.

Notice three things you can hear, like birdsong, traffic sounds, a train, the fridge humming.

Notice two things you can smell, pleasant or unpleasant, such as pine trees or sweat, drying washing or a dog.

Notice one thing you can taste, maybe a drink, or chewing gum.

Do this for a minute or two to help you focus and gain a sense of yourself in your surroundings.

Peace Everyday

Maintaining peace is all about gaining new habits and perceptions and taking care of yourself when you are under pressure. After all, the pressures we face in modern life are not going to diminish; if anything, they're likely to increase. It's how you handle them that makes the difference, and how you do that is down to how you learn to control and channel your mind, your thoughts, your behaviour and your view of yourself.

ENDING NEGATIVE SELF-TALK

Quieten the negative voice in your head by telling yourself the following:

I can decide to quit the negative self-talk.

I will replace it with good thoughts and kind words about myself.

It's completely in my hands.

It is a decision I have the power to make and implement.

It's in my own interest to do it NOW.

CLEAN A SCREEN

Try cleaning your phone, tablet or laptop if you are at work, or a window if you are at home. Take a soft cloth and appropriate cleanser and clean the glass. Start at a corner and work your way across. Give it a good buff up and shine. See how you feel. If you clean a window, look at what you can see outside. Notice how the light reflects.

Calming exercise

FOCUS ON AN OBJECT

Find an object you don't usually look at closely, such as a paperweight, a cushion or a musical instrument. Take a minute to really look at it. Examine the shape, the colour, the form. Hold it if you can. Take it in. Move it to a different place. How do you feel?

Further Resources

Apps
Calm
Headspace
The Mindfulness App
Stop, Breathe & Think

Psychological Help
Action For Happiness (UK)
www.actionforhappiness.org

Barnsbury Therapy Rooms (UK)
www.barnsburytherapyrooms.com

British Association for Counselling and Psychotherapy (BACP) (UK)
www.bacp.co.uk

City Therapy Rooms (UK)
www.citytherapyrooms.co.uk

Counselling Directory (UK)
www.counselling-directory.org.uk

Spectrum Therapy (UK)
www.spectrumtherapy.co.uk

Welldoing (UK)
www.welldoing.org

Mental Health America (US)
www.mhanational.org/get-involved/contact-us

Warmline (US)
www.warmline.org

National Alliance on Mental Illness (US)
www.nami.org

Anxiety and Depression Association of America (ADAA) (USA)
www.adaa.org

The Trevor Project (US)
www.thetrevorproject.org

Depression and Bipolar Support Alliance (US)
www.dbsalliance.org

National Eating Disorder Association (US)
www.nationaleatingdisorders.org

Meditation/Mindfulness

Be Mindful
www.bemindful.co.uk

Breathworks
www.breathworks-mindfulness.org.uk

Mind
www.mind.org.uk

Mindful
www.mindful.org

Samaritans
www.samaritans.org

Sleep

American Sleep Apnea Association
www.sleepapnea.org

Circadian Sleep Disorders Network
www.circadiansleepdisorders.org

Restless Legs Syndrome Foundation
www.rls.org

Narcolepsy Network
www.narcolepsynetwork.org

American Sleep Association
www.sleepassociation.org

Confidence

The Dove Self Esteem Project
www.dove.com/us/en/dove-self-esteem-project.html

The Cybersmile Project
www.cybersmile.org

OneLove
www.joinonelove.org

Loveisrespect
www.loveisrespect.org

Books

The Mindfulness Journal by Corinne Sweet
Pan Macmillan, 2014

The Anxiety Journal by Corinne Sweet
Pan Macmillan, 2017

Full Catastrophe Living: How to cope With stress, pain and illness using mindfulness by Jon Kabat-Zinn
Piatkus, 2013